EXTREME MACHINES

CARS

DAVID JEFFERIS

A+

Smart Apple Media

This book has been published in cooperation with Franklin Watts.

Created for Franklin Watts by Q2A Creative
Editor: Chester Fisher,
Designer: Mini Dhawan,
Picture Researcher: Jyoti Sethi

PICTURE CREDITS
Front cover: DaimlerChrysler, Back cover: vwmpress@motorpics.co.za
pp. 4 middle (National Motor Museum, Beaulieu), 5 top (National Motor Museum, Beaulieu),
6 bottom (National Motor Museum, Beaulieu), 6-7 top (National Motor Museum, Beaulieu),
8 middle (mclaren.com), 8 top (Porsche AG), 10 top (hotrodscustomstuff.com),
10 bottom (Street Rods by Michael, Bill Kyzer), 11 top (Martin Wollny motorsnippets.com),
12-13 bottom (National Motor Museum, Beaulieu), 13 top ('Joker' Hummer pictures supplied
by XoticLimos.Com), 13 middle(go-stretch.com), 14 bottom (Teemu Mottonen/teemu.net),
15 top (DaimlerChrysler), 16 top (Jim Murphy), 17 top (Santa Pod Raceway),
17 middle (Santa Pod Raceway), 18 bottom (Citroën Communication),
19 top (vwmpress@motorpics.co.za), 19 bottom (vwmpress@motorpics.co.za),
20 bottom (Christian Wannyn, Lions Club, Le Bourget, Original at the Palais de
Compiègne, France), 21 top (Jeremy Davey© SSC Programme Ltd), 22 bottom (Eric Seltzer),
23 top (Courtesy of Universal Studios Licencing Inc), 24 top (CARL SCHUPPEL),
25 top (Gibbs Aquada), 26 bottom (David Fewchuk), 27 top (BMW), 27 middle (BMW),
28 top (National Motor Museum, Beaulieu), 28 bottom (National Motor Museum, Beaulieu),
29 top (National Motor Museum, Beaulieu), 29 bottom (mclaren.com).

Published in the United States by Smart Apple Media
2140 Howard Drive West, North Mankato, Minnesota 56003

Library of Congress Cataloging-in-Publication Data

Jefferis, David.
Cars / by David Jefferis.
p. cm. — (Extreme machines)
Includes index.
ISBN-13: 978-1-59920-040-8
1. Automobiles—Juvenile literature. I. Title.

TL147.J44 2007
629.222—dc22   2006030843

9 8 7 6 5 4 3 2 1

CONTENTS

THE FIRST CARS

The age of the car started in 1886 with the three-wheeled "motorwagen" of German inventor Carl Benz.

DAIMLER AND BENZ

The motorwagen was a three-wheeler, but in 1886, another German named Gottlieb Daimler developed a car with four wheels—the layout that has been standard ever since. Both vehicles used the newly-invented gasoline engine.

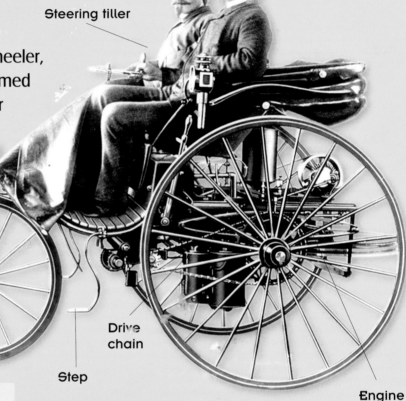

Steering tiller

Drive chain

Step

Engine at back

The Benz three-wheeler had no steering wheel— instead, it had a lever called a tiller.

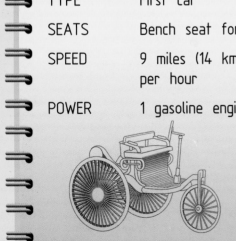

BENZ MOTORWAGEN 1886

TYPE	First car
SEATS	Bench seat for 2
SPEED	9 miles (14 km) per hour
POWER	1 gasoline engine

LONG JOURNEY

In 1888, Benz's wife, Bertha, made the first long-distance car journey between the German towns of Mannheim and Pforzheim. The car was an improved model, but even so the trip took all day and needed several stops for repairs.

In 1906, this Renault won the first French Grand Prix race, covering a distance of 770 miles (1,239 km) in two days.

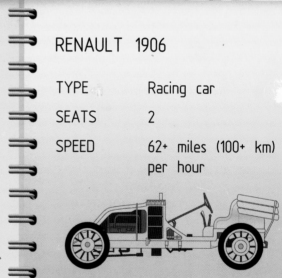

RENAULT 1906

TYPE	Racing car
SEATS	2
SPEED	62+ miles (100+ km) per hour

SPEED KINGS

Soon, there were many other people building cars. They all used speed to show off their new machines. The first official race was held in 1895 between Paris and Bordeaux, France. Soon the world went race-crazy, but the 1903 Paris-Madrid event was a killer—there were so many accidents that the race was stopped and all the cars were sent back to Paris by train!

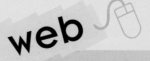

web

FINDER

http://www.mercedesbenz.com
This site provides lots of information on early pioneers. Learn more about early pioneers at the Mercedes Benz museum and read about the company's plans for future cars.

BIG AND SMALL

Most cars are made in standard sizes, usually about 14–18 feet (4.3–5.5 m) long. But a few cars have been made that are very different.

TINY GERMAN

At just over 8.2 feet (2.5 m) long, the Smart FourTwo is the shortest gasoline-powered car in full production. Driving carefully, a Smart driver can expect to travel nearly 70 miles (25 km) per gallon—so the car is very economical, too. The Smart is also easy to park.

The Smart comes in open and closed versions. There is not much room for shopping bags, but two bikes can be carried on a special rack.

Smarts come in patterns as well as plain colors

Plastic body panels

Two seats

SMART FOURTWO

TYPE	Economy micro car
SEATS	2
SPEED	83 miles (134 km) per hour
POWER	3-cylinder gasoline engine

Overall length was 21 feet (6.4 m).

The Bugatti Royale had a silver elephant mascot at the front. The eyes were a pair of red jewels.

The hood was more than 7 feet (1.5 m) long

BUGATTI ROYALE

The Bugatti Royale was designed in the late 1920s and probably has more "extremes" to its name than any other car. It is the most expensive car ever—in 1931, it would have cost $32,000 for one of only six Royales ever made. As an antique, Royales are worth even more. In 1990, a Japanese company paid a staggering $15 million for a Royale!

BUGATTI ROYALE COUPE DE VILLE

TYPE	Luxury car
SEATS	5
SPEED	120 miles (193 km) per hour
POWER	One 8-cylinder gasoline engine

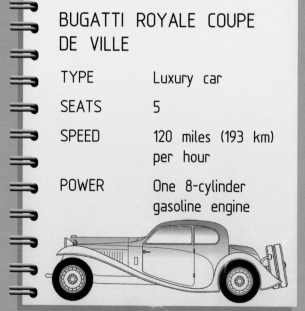

web

FINDER

http://www.ktsmotorsportsgarage.com/rodeo98/pages/bugatti.html
This site has details and pictures of Bugattis and other great classic cars.
http://www.thesmart.co.uk/
Find out about Smart cars at the home site.

SUPERCARS

Supercars have extremely high performance and great looks—and they usually have a high price tag, too!

ULTIMATE CAR?

The first McLaren F1 was sold in 1994 for a mind-boggling $1,203,281. But for this money, a McLaren owner got a car that was extreme in every way, and is still recognized as the one to beat. The acceleration is shattering—the car can accelerate from 0 to 100 miles (161 km) per hour in just 6.3 seconds and its top speed is another record-breaker at 240 miles (386 km) per hour.

McLAREN F1

TYPE	Performance car
SEATS	3
SPEED	240 miles (387 km) per hour, a 1998 record
POWER	1 V-12 gasoline engine

Driver's central seat

Carbon fiber and aluminum alloy

Like other supercars, the McLaren F1 has flip-up "scissor-action" doors.

V-10 engine behind seats

Lightweight carbon fiber and plastic body

Rear spoiler lifts up at high speeds to provide downforce.

The GT can reach 100 miles (161 km) per hour in just 6.9 seconds— almost as quickly as a McLaren F1.

PORSCHE CARRERA GT

TYPE	Performance car
SEATS	2
SPEED	205 miles (330 km) per hour
POWER	1 V-10 gasoline engine

GERMAN CHALLENGE

The Carrera GT is Porsche's attempt at beating the McLaren, though the figures show that it's not quite in the same class. It is slower, at "just" 205 miles (330 km) per hour, and has two seats. Even so, supercar drivers say that the Carrera GT provides most of an F1's performance for half the price, about $612,062.

web

FINDER

http://www.mclarenautomotive.com/homepage.htm
The McLaren site has some great pictures and videos to download.
http://www3.uk.porsche.com/english/gbr/home.htm
Porsche's site gives you facts about all its cars, including the Carrera GT.

EXTREME MACHINES Cars

9

HOT RODS

Hot rods are often made lower at the front than the back, to give them a sportier, racier look.

Hot rods are cars that have been changed or rebuilt to make them faster and better looking.

MIX AND MATCH

Hot rods are often built using parts from a number of different cars. The body of a 1930s Ford Coupe may have brakes from a second car, steering from a third car, and seats from a fourth. Some parts may need to be specially made for the car.

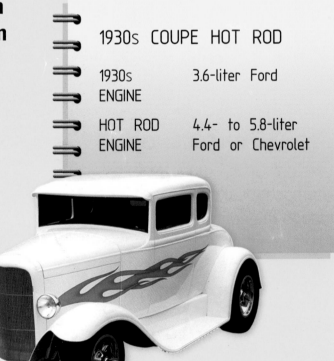

1930s COUPE HOT ROD	
1930s ENGINE	3.6-liter Ford
HOT ROD ENGINE	4.4- to 5.8-liter Ford or Chevrolet

The Pierson Coupe is one of the fastest hot rods ever built.

PIERSON FORD COUPE	
ORIGINAL CAR	1934 Ford Coupe
ENGINE	4.4-liter
1934 TOP SPEED	78 miles (125 km) per hour
HOT ROD TOP SPEED	227 miles (365 km) per hour

RECORD BREAKER

One famous hot rod is called the Pierson Coupe. A coupe is a two-door car with a sloping back. The Pierson Coupe started as an ordinary Ford car made in 1934. It was rebuilt as a super-fast hot rod. It was so fast that it set a number of speed records.

web

FINDER

http://www.streetrodderweb.com/milestones/0106sr_ pierson_brothers_coupe/
Read about the history of the Pierson Coupe hot rod.
http://hotrod.com/featuredvehicles/6042
See more pictures of hot rods and how they are made.

Hot rod owners often participate in rallies. Every car is polished until it gleams!

STRETCH LIMOS

Limousines, or limos, are luxury cars. Stretch limos are limousines that have been made longer.

CUTTING CARS IN TWO

To make a stretch limo, a brand new and very expensive luxury car is cut in two. The cut is made just behind the front seats. Then an extra piece of car body is built in the middle to make the whole car longer.

PUTTING ON WEIGHT

When a car is stretched, it becomes heavier. It may even double in weight. Some of its parts must be replaced because of this extra weight. A car is held up by springs, so stretch limos need stronger springs to support their greater weight. A heavier car is harder to stop, so stretch limos also need more powerful brakes.

LINCOLN TOWN CAR STRETCH LIMO

ENGINE	4.6 l	STRETCHED LENGTH	28 feet (8.5 m)
UNSTRETCHED LENGTH	18 feet (5.5 m)	POWER	239 hp

The Lincoln Town Car is a popular choice for building stretch limos.

This Hummer has been stretched to twice its normal size.

HUMMER H2 STRETCH LIMO

DOORS	5
CAPACITY	20 to 24 people
ENGINE	Vortex 8
UNSTRETCHED LENGTH	15 feet (4.5 m)
STRETCHED LENGTH	30 feet (9 m)

CARS FOR STRETCHING

Luxury Cadillac, Lincoln, and Chrysler cars are the most popular for building stretch limos, but any car can be used. One of the smallest cars in the world, the Mini, has been stretched. There are even stretched versions of military vehicles called Hummers!

web

FINDER

http://www.stretching-it.com/LimoPages/building.htm
See how a stretch limo is built.
http://www.dabryancoach.com/docs/model_detail/120_lincoln.html
See how luxurious a stretch limo is.

A view inside a "stretch" (left).

TOP RACERS

Each year races take place to decide who is the champion driver and car manufacturer. Formula One and NASCAR races are the ultimate tests of car design and driver skills.

PRANCING HORSE

The most famous name in Formula One (F1) is Ferrari from Italy. The firm started in the 1940s and has raced every season since F1 started in 1950. You can spot a Ferrari easily because the cars are always bright red, Italy's traditional racing color, and have Ferrari's "prancing horse" logo on them. Their most famous driver is Michael Schumacher, who has been the World Champion seven times.

FERRARI F2004

TYPE	F1 racing car
SEATS	1
SPEED	190+ miles (306+ km) per hour
POWER	1 V-10 gasoline engine

All F1 cars have a similar look with wide wheels and a powerful engine behind the driver.

Front and rear airfoils force the car down onto the track

Cockpit has a seat made to fit each driver

Wide tires come in "dry" and "wet" versions to suit the weather during a race

A Dodge Intrepid R/T in the NASCAR Winston Cup at the Las Vegas Motor Speedway.

RACING TO WIN

Stock car racing, known as NASCAR, is one of the most popular motor sports in the United States. It began with normal cars being raced around oval-shaped tracks. Today, the cars are specially built for NASCAR races by major manufacturers such as Ford, Chevrolet, Dodge, and Pontiac. There is fierce competition among the teams and drivers at such races as the Daytona 500 to become overall champions of the year. NASCAR races draw huge crowds of more than 100,000 spectators per race.

DODGE INTREPID R/T

TYPE	Road and track car
POWER	5.7-liter, V-8 gasoline engine
SPEED	184 miles (295 km) per hour
DRIVE	Rear wheel

web

FINDER

http://www.thescuderia.net/
This site has lots of information about Ferraris.
Also check *http://www.ferrari.com*.

DRAGSTERS

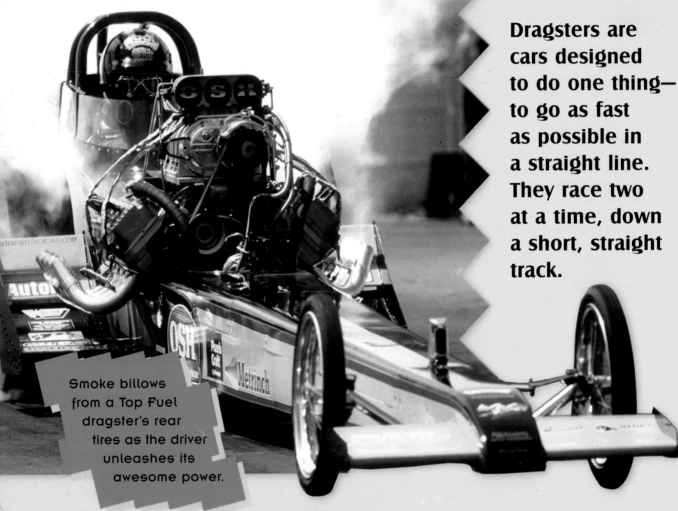

Dragsters are cars designed to do one thing—to go as fast as possible in a straight line. They race two at a time, down a short, straight track.

Smoke billows from a Top Fuel dragster's rear tires as the driver unleashes its awesome power.

AT TOP SPEED!

The fastest dragsters are called Top Fuel dragsters. They burn a fuel called nitromethane in a huge engine at the back of the car. The driver sits in front of this mighty, deafening engine. Top Fuel dragsters reach their top speed in fewer than five seconds—the time it takes for a whole race from start to finish! At the end of a race, they are going so fast that they have to release parachutes to help slow them down.

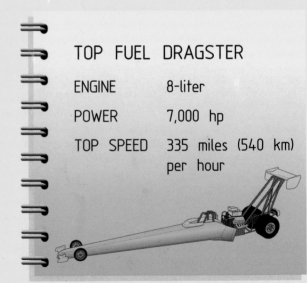

TOP FUEL DRAGSTER

ENGINE	8-liter
POWER	7,000 hp
TOP SPEED	335 miles (540 km) per hour

The driver of this Funny Car is preparing to race at a British speedway.

TOP FUEL FUNNY CAR

ENGINE	8-liter
POWER	7,000 hp
TOP SPEED	333 miles (535 km) per hour

FUNNY CARS

Another type of dragster is the Funny Car. It is covered with a body that looks like an ordinary car. Underneath its body, the engine is the same as a Top Fuel dragster engine, but the Funny Car's engine is in front of the driver. Most Funny Cars are powered by supercharged alcohol engines.

FINDER

http://www.nhra.com/streetlegal/whatisadragrace.html
Find out more about dragsters and drag racing.
http://www.nhra.com/streetlegal/funfacts.html
Read some amazing facts about dragsters and drag racing.

RALLY RACERS

Rallies are long-distance events that take place on roads, dirt tracks, snow, or ice. The cars are similar to those on sale to the public, but they have been adapted for extreme conditions.

WORLD RALLY CHAMPIONSHIP

The World Rally Championship (WRC) takes teams around the world each year in a series of events that last from January to November. But, rallying itself has a long history—the first one was held in 1907, from China to France. The winner took two months to drive 7,500 miles (12,000 km) between Peking and Paris.

KEEPING ON COURSE

To win a rally today, it's essential to have a four-wheel drive (4WD) car so that all the wheels are driven by the engine. With 4WD, cars can scramble around corners quicker and drive through mud or sand more easily.

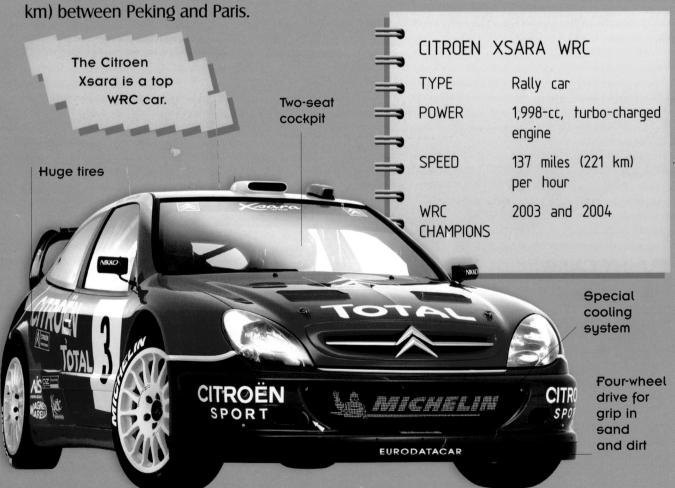

The Citroen Xsara is a top WRC car.

Two-seat cockpit

Huge tires

Special cooling system

Four-wheel drive for grip in sand and dirt

CITROEN XSARA WRC	
TYPE	Rally car
POWER	1,998-cc, turbo-charged engine
SPEED	137 miles (221 km) per hour
WRC CHAMPIONS	2003 and 2004

The Rally Touarag is about as different from the standard car as possible. The standard Touarag is a comfy 4WD car.

DEADLY DAKAR

The most extreme rally of all is the Paris-Dakar, which finishes at Dakar, Senegal. In 2005, it followed a winding route through France, Spain, and four African countries. Special timed stages were held along the way. The Dakar is a dangerous race—accidents are common and drivers are sometimes killed.

VOLKSWAGEN TOUARAG DAKAR

TYPE	Dakar Rally car
SEATS	2 (standard car seats 5 people)
SPEED	130+ miles (209+ km) per hour
POWER	15-cylinder diesel engine

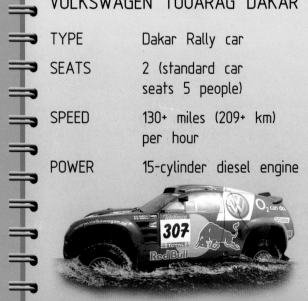

web

FINDER

http://www.wrc.com
The WRC site tells you almost all you need to know about rally cars.
http://www.volkswagen.co.nz/concepts/conceptT/downloads.asp
This Volkswagen site has details of the Touarag and other interesting cars.

SPEED ON WHEELS

Drivers have been trying to smash speed records since the earliest days of the automobile. These two cars were built almost a century apart, but the goal was the same for both—to be fastest in the world.

RED DEVIL

One of the first record-breaking speed drivers was Camille Jenatzy, a Belgian nicknamed "Red Devil" for his extremely long, red beard. In 1898, he put the finishing touches on a bullet-shaped car powered by sets of electric batteries.

NEVER SATISFIED

On May 1, 1899, Jenatzy's electric car, La Jamais Contente ("The Never Satisfied"), became the fastest car in the world when Jenatzy drove it along a track near Paris. His speed at just 66 miles (106 km) per hour may not sound fast today, but it was fast enough to hold the record for three years!

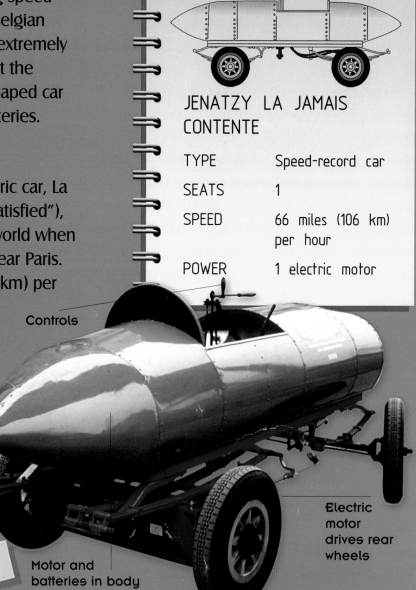

JENATZY LA JAMAIS CONTENTE

TYPE	Speed-record car
SEATS	1
SPEED	66 miles (106 km) per hour
POWER	1 electric motor

Controls

Metal bodywork

La Jamais Contente was the first car to go faster than 62 miles (100 km) per hour.

Electric motor drives rear wheels

Motor and batteries in body

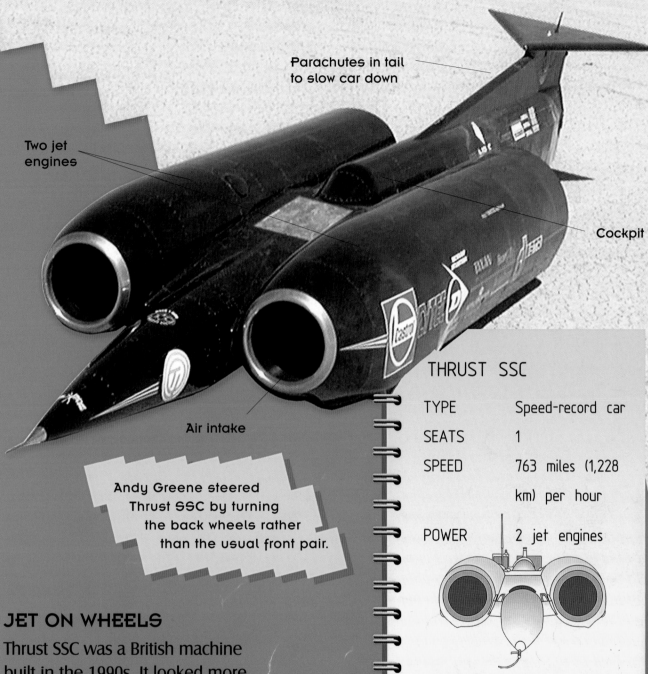

Parachutes in tail
to slow car down

Two jet
engines

Cockpit

Air intake

Andy Greene steered
Thrust SSC by turning
the back wheels rather
than the usual front pair.

THRUST SSC

TYPE	Speed-record car
SEATS	1
SPEED	763 miles (1,228 km) per hour
POWER	2 jet engines

JET ON WHEELS

Thrust SSC was a British machine built in the 1990s. It looked more like a fighter plane than a car, with a sleek tail and two jet engines, one on each side of the needle-nosed body. The driver, Andy Greene, was a jet fighter pilot. In 1997, Thrust SSC broke all records, traveling at almost 763 miles (1,228 km) per hour, hurtling across the flat lands of the Black Rock Desert in Nevada.

web

FINDER

http://www.speedace.info/jamais.htm
This site contains information on speed records, including Jenatzy's.
http://www.thrustssc.com/
Visit the Web site of Thrust SSC for additional details about the car.

STAR CARS

Many extreme cars have been made for television series and Hollywood films. Most are based on real cars, but it is hard to tell after the special effects experts have done their job.

THE BATMOBILE

This is the car that comic-book hero Batman used to chase criminals, first on TV and then in several films. The original TV Batmobile was first shown in 1966. It was converted from a special "concept car," the $250,000 Lincoln Futura made 11 years earlier. This had been built to show what a car of the future might look like.

BATMOBILE (1966 TV SERIES)

TYPE	Crime-fighter car
SEATS	2
SPEED	100+ miles (161+ km) per hour
POWER	1 8-cylinder gasoline engine

The Futura-based Batmobile had fins, rockets, and two aircraft-style cockpit canopies.

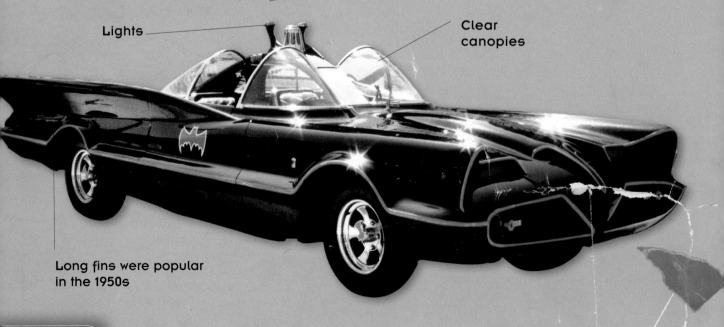

Lights

Clear canopies

Long fins were popular in the 1950s

Gull-wing doors

Extra "time travel" equipment

Only 8,583 DeLoreans were ever made. Amazingly, about 6,000 still survive today. Shown here is the version used in *Back to the Future*.

DELOREAN

The three-film *Back to the Future* series featured the DeLorean car, which was built in 1981–83. In the film, the car could travel in time—only if it hit exactly 88 miles (142 km) per hour! The good-looking original had lift-up "gull wing" doors that made it look futuristic—so all the special effects team had to do was add some technical-looking parts and pieces to make it appear as it did in the movie.

DMC DELOREAN (MOVIE VERSION)

TYPE	Sports car
SEATS	2
SPEED	88 miles (142 km) per hour
POWER	1 8-cylinder gasoline engine + atomic power

web

FINDER

http://www.delorean.com/
This Web site has details of the DeLorean's history and a virtual tour of the company's warehouse.
http://www.bttfmovie.com/
Visit this site to find out about the three *Back to the Future* films.

EXTREME MACHINES Cars

23

WOW WHEELS

Here are some of the most inventive cars ever made, vehicles that test design extremes on water and in the air!

Engine
compartment

Propeller

Two seats
at front

The Taylor
Aerocar had
a "pusher"
propeller
mounted
at the back.

CAR WITH WINGS

The Aerocar was the brainchild of American inventor Moulton Taylor, who designed a small car to which wings and tail could be added when the owner wanted to go flying. Taylor's Aerocar III went on sale in 1956, but was ahead of its time—only six were built. Today there are plans for a brand-new version, based on a Lotus Elize sports car.

PROPELLER POWER

The earlier French Leyat Aerocar also had propeller power, but it had no wings. The 1923 design could reach 100 miles (161 km) per hour on a straight road, but only one was ever made.

TAYLOR AEROCAR III

TYPE	Commuter car plane
SEATS	2
SPEED	On road—70 miles (113 km) per hour; in flight—125 miles (201 km) per hour
POWER	1 Lycoming aircraft engine

Water-jet power
at the back

Fold-up
wheels

The three-seat
Aquada is powerful
enough to tow
a water-skier.

SEA SPEEDER

On land, the Gibbs Aquada looks and drives like any two-seater sports car. In water, the wheels fold away and the Aquada turns into a fast speedboat. The engine squirts a rocket-like jet of water from the back, thrusting the Aquada forward at high speed. It is the world's first high-speed amphibious vehicle. In the 1960's, about 4,000 German Amphibicars were made but they were much slower than the Aquada.

FINDER

http://www.aerocar.com/
Get up-to-date Aerocar developments here.
www.aquada.co.uk
Visit the official Web site of Aquada.

GIBBS AQUADA

TYPE	High-speed, amphibian sports car-boat
SEATS	3
SPEED	On land—100 miles (161 km) per hour; on water—35 miles (56 km) per hour
POWER	1 6-cylinder gasoline engine, which also powers the water-jet

FUTURE CARS

Researchers work hard to make cars better. One goal is to make cars with ultra-clean engines producing little or no pollution.

SUN POWER

Solar cars are the cleanest vehicles of all, using solar panels that change energy from the sun into electricity, which powers electric motors to turn the wheels. To test out new ideas, solar races are held in various countries. In 2005, the Australian Aurora team set several records, including the first solar car to run for 24 hours—the car only stopped to change drivers, repair a flat tire, and fix the radio. To break the record, Aurora's solar panels charged batteries to keep the car going at night.

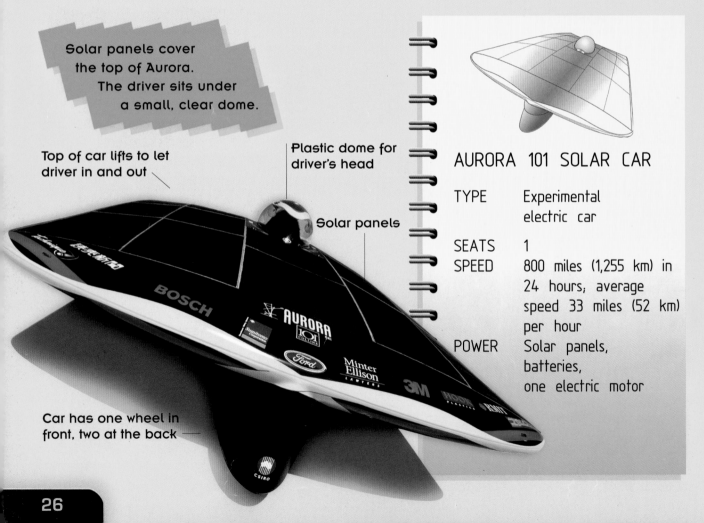

Solar panels cover the top of Aurora. The driver sits under a small, clear dome.

Top of car lifts to let driver in and out

Plastic dome for driver's head

Solar panels

Car has one wheel in front, two at the back

AURORA 101 SOLAR CAR

TYPE	Experimental electric car
SEATS	1
SPEED	800 miles (1,255 km) in 24 hours; average speed 33 miles (52 km) per hour
POWER	Solar panels, batteries, one electric motor

Single-seat cockpit

Lightweight bodywork

Air intake for engine cooling

The H2R engine is based on a standard BMW unit converted to burn hydrogen fuel.

GAS POWER

In Germany, the BMW company is working on an engine that can burn either standard gasoline or hydrogen, a gas which burns so cleanly that its waste is almost entirely water. To test the engine, BMW built the H2R, and in 2005, it broke nine world records for hydrogen cars.

BMW H2R

TYPE	Experimental hydrogen car
SEATS	1
SPEED	186 miles (300 km) per hour
POWER	1 hydrogen-fueled engine

FINDER

http://www.aurorasolarcar.com/
This site shows information on solar power and the Aurora 101 car.
http://www.bmwtransact.com/hydrogen/cars_h2r.htm
Visit this site to check out BMW's hydrogen-fuel research.

TIMELINE

1886

First successful gasoline-powered cars are developed by Carl Benz (a three-wheel design) and Gottlieb Daimler (four-wheel design) in Germany.

1888

Bertha Benz becomes the first woman driver and makes the first long-distance journey by car, taking her two sons, Eugen and Richard, on the 61-mile (100 km) trip.

1895

First big car race held, from Paris to Bordeaux and back. It was won by Emile Lavassor, driving a Panhard. He averaged 15 miles (24 km) per hour over the 732-mile (1,178 km) course. This was an amazing feat—at the time, cars were unreliable and most roads were no better than dusty or muddy trails.

1896

First race on a closed circuit held in Rhode Island. Cars raced for five laps around a 1-mile (1.6 km), dirt and cinder track in a park. An electric car won the race.

1903

First big racing accidents during the Paris-to-Madrid race, which stopped before the drivers had even left France. The only female driver was Madame du Gast who became a heroine for stopping to help injured drivers.

1905

Tourist Trophy race held on Isle of Man. It is still held every year and is the oldest race running.

1907

First long-distance rally held, from China to Britain. The rally was repeated in 1990, but this time the direction was reversed, from London to Beijing!

1908

Ford Model T "Tin Lizzie" goes on sale. From the start, the car was a success and by 1922 one million were being made every year.

1927

The Ford Model T is replaced by the improved Ford Model A.

1937

Design completed for the Volkswagen (VW) Beetle, as an inexpensive "people's car." The Beetle holds the record for biggest production of the same design, at more than 21 million when VW stopped making it in 2003.

1958

Ford Edsel launched in the U.S. and was considered to be the biggest failure ever, because Ford lost about $300 million on the car. Today, an Edsel is a highly-prized classic car!

1959

Bruce McLaren from New Zealand becomes the youngest Grand Prix (GP) winner after taking the lead at the U.S. Grand Prix in Florida. The oldest GP winner was Tazio Nuvolari, an Italian driver who won the French Grand Prix in 1946 when he was 53 years old.

1969

Closest Le Mans win, when drivers of a Ford GT40 and Porsche 908 battled for victory. After 24 hours racing, the GT40 won by only 328 feet (100 m)!

1977

Longest rally held, from London to Sydney. Distance covered was 19,329 miles (31,107 km). Today's rallies are usually shorter, but the World Rally Championship (WRC) is a hard-fought set of rallies during a year. It's considered to be at least as tough as any longer, single rally held in the past.

1992

McLaren F1 launched as the most powerful production car ever made. Six years later the car was still setting records—in 1998, it reached 240.1 miles (386.7 km) per hour at a test track in Germany.

1999

White Lightning Electric Streamliner is driven at 245.523 miles (395.821 km) per hour to become the world's fastest electric vehicle. White Lightning was driven by Patrick Rummerfield at the Bonneville Salt Flats in Utah.

2004

Enzo is Ferrari's most expensive performance car for sale. Without extras, the cost is $792,456! The Mercedes SLR McLaren is a close competitor if you have the money—painted only black or silver, the car can go from a standstill to 62 miles (100 km) per hour in just 3.8 seconds, and costs about $596,903!

2005

Aurora solar-electric car record is taken for going continuously for 24 hours, even at night, when the car continues using batteries that were charged during daylight hours.

GLOSSARY

AIRFOIL

A wing-like fin on a performance car that helps keep it firmly on the road or track by using the push of passing air to create a downward pressure called down-force.

ALUMINUM

A light but strong metal used for construction.

AMPHIBIOUS CAR

A car that can travel on water as well as land.

CARBON FIBER

A plastic material with fibers of carbon added during manufacturing. It is very light and strong, so it is used a lot for racing cars.

CIRCUIT

A track used for racing that is not open for other vehicles. A few circuits, such as Le Mans, have some parts of the circuit that are public roads, but these are closed to traffic on race days.

COCKPIT

Part of the car where the crew sit—may have one or two seats depending on the car.

CONCEPT CAR

A one-of-a-kind futuristic, experimental car usually appearing at motor shows to stimulate interest in the manufacturer's products. Concept cars push car design forward, but only a few reach the production stage.

CUSTOM CAR

A standard model of car that has been adapted by its owner to make it look or drive the way he or she wants it.

DIESEL ENGINE

A type of internal-combustion engine that burns thick diesel instead of gasoline *(see gasoline engine).*

DRAG RACER

A car that has been specially designed to take in short, high-speed acceleration races.

FORMULA

Set of rules that apply to a particular kind of racing. The formula controls how a car is made, the size of its engine, its weight and many other details.

FOUR-WHEEL DRIVE (4WD)

A system that transfers engine power to all four wheels. 4WD provides superior traction compared with front- or rear-wheel drive.

GASOLINE

A liquid made from oil that burns easily and is the main fuel for internal-combustion engines.

GASOLINE ENGINE

Type of engine that uses gasoline as its fuel. The engine itself is called an internal-combustion (ic) engine, because it burns fuel in cylinders inside the engine. The cylinders can vary in number and arrangement, from simple ones such as 4 in-line to complex designs such as V-12.

GRAND PRIX

French words for "grand prize" and mostly used when talking about Formula One racing.

HORSEPOWER (HP)

The unit for measuring the power output of an engine. Higher horsepower increases the vehicle's top speed. One horsepower is defined as lifting 33,000 pounds one foot per minute. The term was first used by the inventor James Watt when he wanted to compare the power of a steam engine to that of the horse it replaced.

HOT ROD

Any car that has been rebuilt or modified to increase its speed and acceleration.

HYDROGEN

Flammable gas used in some experimental engines, such as the BMW H2R.

INTERNAL-COMBUSTION ENGINE

Any engine in which the fuel is consumed in the interior of the engine rather than outside of the engine.

NASCAR

National Association for Stock Car Auto Racing. The organization that promotes and regulates stock-car racing in the U.S.

POLLUTION

Chemical waste in the unburned parts of a car exhaust. Today's engines produce much less pollution than earlier types, and future engines should make even less.

SOLAR CELL

Silicon material that changes the energy in sunlight to electricity. Solar cells are usually made in the form of thin, flat panels that can be laid out to catch the Sun's rays.

SPONSOR

A company that pays a racing team for advertising its products on the cars.

STAGE

A specially timed section of a rally. On stages, cars normally leave at one-minute intervals, with crews aiming to finish at an exact time. They lose points if they are late and often, if they are early too.

Note to parents and teachers:
Every effort has been made to ensure that the Web sites in this book are suitable for children, that they are of the highest educational value, and that they contain no inappropriate or offensive material. However, because of the nature of the Internet, it is impossible to guarantee that the contents of these sites will not be altered. We strongly advise that Internet access be supervised by a responsible adult.

INDEX